DEFENCE

OF THE

RIGHT AND THE DUTY

OF THE

AMERICAN UNION

TO IMPROVE ITS

NAVIGABLE WATERS,

IN

A SPEECH

BY

SAMUEL B. RUGGLES,

AT

CONSTITUTION HALL, IN THE CITY OF NEW YORK,

OCTOBER 8, 1852.

NEW YORK:
BAKER, GODWIN & CO., PRINTERS,
CORNER NASSAU AND SPRUCE STREETS.
1852.

DEFENCE

OF THE RIGHT AND THE DUTY OF THE

AMERICAN UNION

TO IMPROVE ITS

NAVIGABLE WATERS.

IN A SPEECH BY

SAMUEL B. RUGGLES,

AT CONSTITUTION HALL, IN THE CITY OF NEW YORK,

OCTOBER 8, 1852.

A MEETING was held, on the evening of the 8th October, 1852, at CONSTITUTION HALL, in the city of New York, for the purpose of hearing an address from SAMUEL B. RUGGLES, Esq., upon the subject of the Improvement of Rivers and Harbors, by the National Government. The meeting was called in consequence of the compliance of Mr. RUGGLES with the request conveyed in the following letter:

NEW YORK, Tuesday, Oct, 5, 1852.

HON. SAMUEL B. RUGGLES—*Dear Sir:* Among the issues of the pending Presidential Canvass, our city has special interest in that which relates to the duty of the National Government to aid the National Commerce, by the improvement of our Rivers and Harbors.

We take the liberty, on behalf of a large number of our fellow-citizens, to request that you will address them upon this subject at as early a day as may suit your convenience. Your former connection with this matter as President of the Board of Commissioners of the Canals of this great State,—works truly national in their relations,—the distinguished abilities which you brought to the discharge of the duties of that high position, and the general interest which you have always manifested in the subject, lead us to look to you with confidence for information upon it which may be useful in the coming contest.

Trusting that you may find it convenient to comply with our wishes in this respect.

We are, very truly, your obedient servants,

DANIEL LORD,	CHARLES KING,
JAMES G. KING,	SIMEON DRAPER,
WM. B. ASTOR,	J. J. ASTOR,
C. AUGUSTUS DAVIS,	H. J. RAYMOND,
GEORGE W. BLUNT,	MOSES MAYNARD, Jr.,
JOHN WARD,	A. WAKEMAN,

(and many others.)

The meeting was organized by the appointment of CHARLES AUGUSTUS DAVIS, Esq., Chairman, and GEORGE W. BLUNT, Esq., Secretary.

The letter of invitation having been read, Mr. RUGGLES addressed the meeting, as follows:

MR. CHAIRMAN AND GENTLEMEN: I am here this evening, upon your kind invitation, to address you on the subject of the improvement, by the Government of the United States, of the Rivers and Harbors, required for the safety of our National Commerce.

The flattering manner in which you have referred to my former connection with the public works of this State, deserves my grateful acknowledgements; and I beg to assure you, that any efforts I may have made to hasten the completion of these great channels of commercial intercourse, are more than repaid by this proof of your regard. I hope that you will permit me to add, in justice to myself, that these efforts never had any personal object, beyond the satisfaction of contributing, in some small measure, to the general good.

The proper improvement of the great navigable waters of the Union, to render them safe and convenient for its rapidly expanding commerce, is a subject highly important to the American People. It ought to be above and beyond all party conflicts; but I regret to perceive that it is deeply involved in the approaching Presidential Election.

The Whig party, to which we belong, have now been urging, for many years, the improvement of our Rivers and Harbors by the National Government. Their opponents deny such improvements to be constitutional or necessary, or claim that, if necessary at all, they should be made solely by the separate States.

It was some years, before the issue on this question was presented in the precise form I have above stated; but recent events have brought it distinctly in this shape before the American people; and it now forms the most prominent, among the features which distinguish the contending parties. In discussing the merits of the candidates now before us, I shall therefore seek to confine myself strictly to the attitude they respectively occupy, in relation to this great question. Above all I shall endeavor to avoid personalities, and shall cheerfully follow the example recently set by General Cass, one of the most eminent of our opponents, and admit at once that both the candidates are men of patriotism and honor.

The fundamental position taken by the Whigs, who claim that the Nation should make the necessary River and Harbor improvements, is that the navigable waters of the United States, for all purposes of commerce known to the Constitution, are national waters. On the other hand, our opponents contend that those waters are not national, but local, and that their improvement should be exclusively committed to the respective States. They further propose that, for the purpose of such local improvements, Congress should now consent that each State may lay tonnage duties on that portion of our navigable waters falling within its limits. It is this latter proposition, comparatively of recent origin, which we deem particularly destructive and alarming, and we oppose it not only as impracticable and inexpedient, but as unjust, unconstitutional, and denationalizing.

For what is the Nation of which we are a part? What are its navigable waters? What is its commerce? What is its Constitution? And what rights does that Constitution confer, and what obligations does it impose, in respect to the national commerce?

The Nation occupies an important portion of the earth, and stands among the great continental powers of the civilized world. Embracing twenty degrees of latitude in the temperate zone of the North American Continent, and stretching through nearly sixty degrees of longitude from the Atlantic to the Pacific, it covers the whole Continental expanse within those vast limits. In territorial area, it is now nearly as large as Europe; but running down to the verge of the tropics, it has a much greater variety of climate and culture, and far exceeds the whole of Europe in every element of continental strength.

It has more ready access than Europe to the two oceans—the great highways of the globe—and lying ten degrees nearer the equator, its geographical position, in any great national or commercial struggle, will be much more convenient and commanding.

But in one all-important respect, it very far exceeds Europe; for it has, what Europe has not—one vast, unbroken chain of navigable waters, overspreading its interior, and nearly covering its whole territorial area, binding all its portions in commercial and political unity, and thus concentrating to a degree the world sees nowhere else, the national power of a continent.

In the providence of God, this great portion of the earth has been committed to our care. Let us, therefore, look at it a little more minutely, and see what it contains.

We find it to be about three thousand miles wide, of which two thousand are spread out in one vast plain, lying nearly midway between the two oceans. This plain is separated by the Alleghany Mountains on the East from the Atlantic, and by the Rocky Mountains on the West from the Pacific. The remaining portions of the Continent, which are comparatively mere fragments, consist of a narrow belt, less than two hundred miles wide, between the Alleghanies and the Atlantic, and a broader belt about eight hundred miles wide between the Rocky Mountains and the Pacific.

This plain is drained by one great river, and it is so nearly level with the surface of the earth, that the river and all its tributaries are susceptible of unbroken navigation. The great valley which they drain is not only of unequalled agricultural fertility, but in its unrivalled capacity for inland commerce, it possesses the vital element which must make it dominant, as the central seat of empire.

The great problem, therefore, for us, the American people, to work out, was to connect this valley by adequate means of commercial intercourse, first with the Atlantic, and, in due time, with the Pacific.

The first step in the process has been accomplished. Employing as parts of the system the great chain of lakes, which lie on the North-eastern border of the valley, we have constructed artificial channels, which connect the Mississippi in an unbroken line of navigation with the Atlantic, so that streams of inland trade, secure from foreign aggression, and, as yet, from local interference, are flowing throughout all our territory lying east of the Rocky Mountains.

The history of this nation, which now covers little more than two hundred years, discloses two important facts. First—that Providence has undoubtedly designed to build up on this Western Hemisphere, one great, homogeneous Power; and next, that the navigable waters of the United States, and the Constitution of the United States, are the two great instrumentalities by which that design is to be effected. Our history forms only a part in that great progress; but it has carried us to a point, from which we can clearly survey the past and, to some extent, discern the future.

Without attempting any minute historical detail, we may say, generally, that America was civilized bv several European nations, of different tongue and race. Spain seized the South, France the North, England the middle which, was itself subdivided into thirteen separate colonies; and Holland and Sweden each attempted to snatch a part, but were soon displaced. For more than a hundred years, France not only kept its portion, but added to it the whole of the Mississippi valley. Men are yet living, who have seen the territory, now occupied by this nation, divided among these three European powers. In 1763, France surrendered its portion to England, and twenty years afterwards, in 1783, England surrendered to its thirteen colonies, then become States, all between the Atlantic and the Mississippi. By subsequent negotiations, within the last fifty years, they have acquired the residue between the Mississippi and the Pacific.

By these successive operations, the motley groups of European colonists that came out two hundred years ago to divide this continent, have been fused into one common mass, and the Continent of America now stands united before the world.

The most curious feature in this progress, is the slow rate at which we first advanced. To us of the present hour, somewhat accustomed to the giant pace with which the nation makes its way, the fact is hardly credible that, after sixty years of struggle, the Pilgrims of Massachusetts found their western frontier on the Connecticut River, while all the energies of the New-Netherlands could push the Dutchmen no further west than the Mohawk, sixteen miles from Albany.

In fact, down to the breaking out of the American Revolution, and up to its close, very little was known of America west of the Alleghanies. The thirteen colonies, thinly sprinkled along the narrow belt between the mountains and the Atlantic, looked almost exclusively to the ocean, for the means of commercial intercourse. They dealt mainly with the parent State, very little with each other, and not at all with the great interior beyond the Alleghanies. Not a carriage road of any description led into it; and it lay at the peace of 1783, a vast wilderness, all but unbroken, through which the Mississippi and its tributaries were flowing in solitude, undisturbed by civilized man.

But the moment the peace of 1783 extended the Western boundary of the United States to that river, the men of the day began to turn their attention to this great acquisition. They had gone through the Revolution, under certain Articles of Confederation, intended mainly for military purposes, and which had worked badly enough even in that respect. Their affairs were managed by a Federal Congress, in which each State had a vote. An ordinance was introduced into that body by Mr. Jefferson, in 1784, for the government of a portion of the territory beyond the mountains, but it was wholly silent on the subject of commerce or navigation.

And now the Mississippi is first seen, dimly foreshadowing its future power as a great element of American unity. Some of our statesmen caught glimpses not only of its geographical extent, and the wide-spread development of its valley, but also of its vital political importance, as a great seat of empire and perpetual bond of National Union. But a stream possessing such power and attributes was a new fact in the history of human civilization. In Asia, the eagle eye of ALEXANDER the Great may have seen something a little like it in the Indus, but Western Europe afforded no example. Its scanty and ragged peninsulas projecting into the Atlantic from the Eastern Continent, could hold no such basin. The two small British Islands dismembered from that Continent, furnished us language and laws, but no idea of a river.

But even the trifling streams of Europe were not wholly without instruction. In England, the tyranny of King JOHN six hundred years ago, in obstructing some of their little rivers, led the bold reformers at Runnymede to insert "freedom of rivers" as a fundamental clause in Magna Charta; while on the Continent, darkened by diplomacy, the treaty of Westphalia in 1648, deliberately locked up the navigation of the Scheldt, a valuable commercial stream leading into the German Ocean, and in the face of civilized Christian Europe, kept it locked up nearly a century and a half.

It was under the salutary instruction thus afforded by the Scheldt, and just before the French Revolution broke its shackles, that our thirteen Confederated States acquired the Mississippi.

In March, 1785, RUFUS KING, then a delegate from Massachusetts in the Congress of the Confederation, received from TIMOTHY PICKERING a letter containing these emphatic and memorable words:

"The water communications in that country will always be in the highest degree interesting to the inhabitants. It seems very necessary to secure the *freedom of navigating* these to *all the inhabitants of all the States.* I hope we shall have no *Scheldts* in that country."

The high duty of carrying into effect that great suggestion, immediately occupied the attention of Mr. KING and his associates. The honor of framing the clause—which secures, "not for a day, but for all time," freedom of commerce over an unbroken net-work of navigable water spread out for more than sixteen thousand miles—was shared between Massachusetts and Virginia, then standing shoulder to shoulder, where they had stood throughout the Revolution.

The clause was formally introduced into the Congress by Mr. GRAYSON, of Virginia, and seconded by Mr. KING, of Massachusetts. Listen to its words, so broadly national, so purely American:

"The navigable waters leading into the Mississippi and St. Lawrence, and the carrying places between the same, shall be *common property*, and FOREVER FREE, as well to the inhabitants of the said country, as to the citizens of the United States, and those of any other States that may be admitted into the Confederacy—WITHOUT ANY TAX, DUTY OR IMPOST THEREFOR."

The clause was immediately incorporated into the ordinance, and passed by the Congress on the 13th day of July, 1787.

Here, then, we behold the Magna Charta of the internal navigation of America. It throws its protecting mantle not only over the magnificent area drained by the Mississippi and all its tributaries, but covers with its ample folds the whole basin of the St. Lawrence, with its chain of inland seas; and, as if prophetic of the labors of posterity, it smooths the way, by securing perpetual freedom even to the land portages, or carrying places, between those two great systems of waters. The precursor of the Constitution, it was built on a basis too broad to be displaced, even by that majestic structure. It was never superseded, modified, or weakened, but it was taken bodily into the very frame-work of the Constitution, which came into being, expressly subject to its immutable obligation. The whole power of the Union is incompetent to abate one jot or tittle of this fundamental compact, pre-existing at its birth, and destined to endure forever.

The Articles of Confederation had no regard whatever to commerce. On the contrary, they distinctly prohibited the Confederation from interfering in any way, even by treaties with foreign nations, with the power of the separate States to levy separate duties at their sole discretion. The only semblance of commercial power conferred by the Articles, is a permission to regulate trade with the Indians—and not even with them, should they reside within the limits of a State. In that disjointed and semi-barbarous state, the Confederation came out of the Revolution.

The melancholy condition of the nominally confederated, but really disunited States, during the four years succeeding the peace of 1783, is too well known. It is truly the most discreditable, if not the most painful period of our history. Amid all its demoralizations and abuses, nothing was more conspicuous than the commercial rivalries and disturbances, of which our navigable waters became the theatre. Commerce and navigation having no common head, and the States no longer threatened by a common enemy, they were fast lapsing into the worst condition of the petty Republics of the middle ages; and those who had studied the politics only of disunited Europe, confidently predicted wasting civil war, which would eventually compel the exhausted parties to return to the common protection of the British monarch.

The Chesapeake, divided between Maryland and Virginia, each claiming to levy separate duties on its commerce, became the scene of constant disorder while New York and New Jersey disputed for the Hudson. In the vivid language of the day, as quoted by Mr. Madison, "New Jersey, placed between Philadelphia and New York, was a cask, tapped at both ends; and North Carolina, between Virginia and South Carolina, a patient bleeding at both arms."

The Chesapeake, however, has the honor of being the first to bring the disputants to their senses. The feeble Confederation being wholly helpless and unable to provide a remedy, a Convention, called by several of the separate States, to consider the disorders prevailing on the Chesapeake, assembled at Annapolis. It is enough to say that ALEXANDER HAMILTON, of New York, was there, and saw the full value of the occasion—that his clear intellect and transcendant genius, at once acute and comprehensive, discerned in our navigable waters the key to a political union of the discordant States.

With consummate sagacity he built upon this foundation, and in the second convention which assembled soon afterwards, with enlarged powers, at Philadelphia, he introduced into the Constitution the great commercial clause, which makes it imperishable. Far be it from me to undervalue the other splendid manifestations of creative power, exhibited in that matchless instrument—its novel and felicitous intermixture of the Federal with the National element—the perfection and harmony of its component parts—its massive strength, yet faultless symmetry—and above all, its freedom from geographical trammels, permitting the indefinite expansion, yet perfect security of the Great Nation it called into being; but all these excellences would have been unavailing but for the one all-controlling, all-pervading power over commerce, which united and nationalized our vast navigable waters, and made them one and indivisible forever.

On the 4th day of March, 1789, the Old Thirteen States ceased to be confederated and became united. The first sentence of the Constitution announced to mankind, that the people of these Thirteen States had entered into a more perfect Union. The 4th of July, 1776, had proclaimed the independence of thirteen separate States; but the 4th of March, 1789, was the birth day of the Nation—for then it first came into the world with a nation's form and features, and all the proper functions of a nation.

The Confederation was an old idea, borrowed from Europe, but the Union was purely American.

The great novelty of the American Constitution consists in the skillful distribution of the necessary powers of government between the Nation and the States which compose it. Appropriating no power rightfully belonging to the separate States and necessary for the regulation of their local affairs and peculiar institutions, it confers upon the Nation only those great attributes of sovereignty, needed for the due enjoyment and proper preservation of its own existence. And thus we have a limited, national government, the first the world ever saw—limited, not in its powers—as is sometimes inaccurately stated—but in the number and nature of its powers. In the exercise of the several powers which are expressly granted and enumerated, it cannot be limited. It must be supreme. For who would call the power "to raise and support armies," or "to provide and maintain a navy," a limitedpower?

And so of the power in question, "to regulate commerce"—is any limit imposed on the power to regulate? Can any authority other than that of the

Union regulate commerce with foreign nations oramong the States? Is not the power to "regulate" exclusive, by the mere force of the term itself? How is it possible for more than one authority to regulate the same thing, at the same time?

The only sensible inquiry must be, what is a regulation of commerce, and what does it embrace?

And here we need not waste time upon verbal subtleties or metaphysical abstractions. We leave hair-splitting to those happy regions where the faculty for that pursuit is more fully developed. But we do ask, and insist that a little common sense shall be employed in constructing the National Constitution. We look up to it as a great and beneficent instrument—almost a gift of God himself; and we claim in its behalf, that it shall be fairly and honestly interpreted, in its true substance and plain intent.

If we distinctly understand the position taken by those who deny the power of the National Government to regulate commerce, by improving rivers, or constructing harbors or other works necessary for its security, it is this: That the power to "regulate commerce" denotes only the power to regulate the rates of impost and duty to be laid upon it, and of restraining any separate State from laying any such duty or impost; in a word, that regulation means something abstract and invisible, and does not embrace anything physical or visible.

Now, in answer to this, we would urge that the word "regulate" is of all others, the one conveying the broadest possible signification, covering every imaginable mode of action, visible or invisible. For that very reason it was selected by those who framed the Constitution. The great architects who reared that structure were no ordinary workmen. They well knew the size and the strength of the words they were using. They laid their work in huge blocks, that it might last forever.

If we examine the Constitution, we find that a prior section had already given to Congress the power of laying duties and imposts, and that another section expressly prohibited the separate States from doing so. No imaginable reason could exist for introducing a fresh clause again conferring the same power, and enforcing the same prohibition, and that, too, by a mere implication. The style of the Constitution is quite too faultless, to leave it possible that its authors could introduce any such superfluity or surplusage.

But leaving this examination of the mere words—the hollow shell of the Constitution—we shall contend, that neither its framers nor the American people could ever have intended to leave the Government without the power to regulate commerce, and that, too, by physical and visible means; that it was indispensably necessary for the Government thus to exercise it; that the Government, in fact, has constantly done so from its organization to the present moment; and that this long, uninterrupted, and all but unquestioned usage, has now settled and firmly established the constitutional doctrine, that the power to regulate commerce includes the power to do so practically, by affording such physical facilities as are needful for its existence, safety and convenience.

For let us look back, and see what commerce did in fact require, and what the Government has done.

GEORGE WASHINGTON took the oath of office, as the first President of the United States, in the City of New-York, the 4th of March, 1789. It is true that he had been a "military chieftain," but he certainly would be the last to assume unlawful power.

Now, it so happens that almost the first, if not the very first, of his official acts, was to regulate commerce, and that, too, in the very mode for which we contend.

A light-house was then standing on Sandy Hook, almost within his very sight. It had been erected in 1762, by Royal or Colonial authority. Four or five other lights had also been placed at distant points, on the rocky coast of New England. Upon the long, sandy shore, stretching for nearly seven hundred miles, from New-York to Charleston, but one solitary light was burning. The rickety old Confederation found no Federal authority for upholding structures of that description, and the continent virtually lay buried in darkness.

A letter is now in existence in the proper hand-writing of GEORGE WASHINGTON, written soon after he took the oath of office, directing the keeper of Sandy Hook Light to keep it burning, until Congress should take it especially under their charge.

The first Congress, embracing among their number the very fathers of the Republic, hastened to exercise their constitutional duty. The law of April 7, 1789, being their ninth act, promptly and comprehensively provided, "that all expenses incurred before its passage, for the necessary support, maintenance, and repairs of all light-houses, beacons, buoys, and for the piers erected, placed, or sunk, at the entrance of, or within any bay, inlet, harbor or port *of the United States*, for rendering the navigation thereof easy and safe, shall be defrayed out of the Treasury of the United States."

Regarding the Chesapeake Bay, as a portion of the waters of the United States, it then directs a light-house to be erected near its entrance; and thus, the ancient soil of Virginia saw the first national work for the regulation of commerce, erected by the government of this Union. I am painfully aware, that the rapid extension of these structures, has seriously disturbed the abstract meditations of some of the political philosophers of that venerable commonwealth; but nevertheless, lights and light-houses have made their way, until the whole Atlantic coast is illuminated from the St. Croix to the Rio Grande. In all the political mutations we have undergone during the last sixty years, no party has been found strong enough, or barbarous enough, to prevent the Government from erecting and upholding these structures. But where in all that long period, did it find the constitutional authority, if not in the power to regulate commerce?

In truth, the existence of such a power is irresistibly deducible, from the absolute and evident necessity for its exercise. The Constitution denied it to the States. Could it intend to leave the Government without the power? Could a Christian community exist and stand erect, in the family of civilized nations, and shroud its shores in utter darkness? For what do we see when we look around us? The British Islands blazing with upwards of three hundred lights—France with more than one hundred and fifty—the Baltic, the Mediterranean, the Euxine, all illuminated; and even in the frozen North, Imperial Russia lighting the American mariner on his pathway through the White Sea, out to the Polar Basin. The whole globe from North to South, from East to West, is encircled with these living monuments of humanity and civilization. And could America, young and vigorous America, refuse to lend its hand to such a work?

In 1801, THOMAS JEFFERSON became the President of the United States. If any one expects from me any disrespect to the memory of that distinguished man, he will be disappointed. I am aware, that among the numerous and often fugitive writings, coming from his prolific pen, at different periods of his life, passages may possibly be found, which would narrow the powers, not only of the government of the Union, but of all other governments of every description. It may even be true, that some of his political suggestions would not wholly suit a country so progressive as ours. They certainly would not harmonize with some of the greatest acts of his own administration. For who will deny, that the acquisition of Louisiana was greatest of them all?—and yet this signal act of statesmanship, was only the exercise by Mr. JEFFERSON, of the constitutional power to facilitate and protect, and in that way to regulate the commerce of the Union.

Louisiana, originally colonized by France, had been temporally transferred to Spain. Experience has sufficiently taught the two Americas the effects of Spanish dominion upon human progress. The Plata, the Amazon, the Oronoco, have fully told the story in one of the Continents, and the Mississippi might have told it in the other.

Suffice it to say, that about the time Mr. JEFFERSON's accession to office, the American people, then just beginning to descend the western slope of the Alleghanies, found their access to the Gulf of Mexico through the Mississippi, obstructed not only by snags and sandbars, as at present, but by an impediment still worse—a Spanish governor at its mouth, occupying the port of New Orleans.

Steam had not then entered the world to subdue its waters, and not a vessel was seen throughout the whole length of the Mississippi, but Indian canoes and occasionally a barge or Mackinaw boat laden with furs, and drifting down the current.

But even this infant commerce Mr. JEFFERSON deemed it his duty to regulate, protect, and facilitate, and that too with no feeble hand. Earnest efforts were made, not for the purpose of removing the physical impediments in the stream, for in the then existing state of the navigation they were less important, but to buy from Spain the port of New Orleans outright. But entreaties and even threats were unavailing, and we should certainly have gone to war, for the sole purpose of obtaining the necessary facilities which our inland trade required, but for the fortunate retrocession of the colony to France. To the Government of that country, at that time controlled by NAPOLEON, Mr. JEFFERSON immediately sent out special ministers instructed to purchase New Orleans—surely not for the purpose of adding to our territory, for every one thought we had enough—but solely to secure this indispensable appendage to our inland commerce. Now, was not this something physical and visible?—something beyond the abstract, invisible, and merely legal power to regulate commerce by adjusting the rates of duties and imposts?

Mr. JEFFERSON did not at first succeed. NAPOLEON refused to sell New Orleans, unless the whole of Louisiana from the Mississippi to the Pacific were purchased with it. "The whole or none," were his terms. Our ministers sent home for fresh authority, which Mr. JEFFERSON promptly gave, and the whole was purchased for sixteen millions of dollars. Looking at it now, it was not dear, and would not have been at twenty times the cost. But where was there a word in the Constitution, giving a semblance of authority to buy it, save in the vast and beneficent power to regulate commerce with foreign nations and among the several States?

The annexation of this vast domain to the pre-existing territory of the United States, vitally altered, not only the relations of the States, one to the other, but also the relative position of the nation to the great powers of the world. The change, not then so apparent, is now obvious to us all. The United States of America then became Continental America, not only in name but in fact. She stood before the world one of its imperial powers, uniting for all the purposes of national sovereignty, the continent between the Atlantic and the Pacific.

Now let us look at our system of navigable waters, as modified by this cardinal fact in our civil history—the doubling of our territorial extent—and I do not ask you to do this for any idle purpose of historical inquiry, but for the sake of stating a fundamental proposition which directly concerns the matter in hand, and which I shall seek to prove, which is, that by that great event, the constitutional responsibilities of the National Government, in respect to the regulation of commerce on its navigable waters, were almost immeasurably increased.

It is not that the political supremacy of the States on the Atlantic was then extinguished,—for thanks to our glorious Constitution, it has taught us to know no East, no West,—but it is, that the immense commerce called into being, by the concentration then effected of all the waters of the Mississippi under one common authority, renders that of the Atlantic comparatively insignificant.

The commercial movement on the Atlantic we all know, for figures measure it, but who will count the movement of the Mississippi, when its valley shall be fully peopled? Can the broken, discordant fragments of disunited Europe furnish us the rule? Why, the Mississippi valley, if laid down upon the map of Europe, would all but cover every kingdom, principality and power it contains, "*patches*" and all, from Cadiz to the Russian frontier! We may know the aggregate length of the river and its navigable tributaries, for our engineers tell us it is sixteen thousand seven hundred miles,—a line long enough to encircle Europe, and leave a remnant which would span the Atlantic; but who will measure the gigantic mass of the products, which sixteen thousand seven hundred miles of navigable water, spread out in one unbroken net-work, will receive from populations united by millions and tens of millions, and concentrating all their commerce in a single channel?

My friends, the interior was becoming too large. Space was becoming inconvenient, if not dangerous; and it was time for ROBERT FULTON to come into the world and build a steamboat; and so he did, in 1807, four years after Mr. JEFFERSON bought Louisiana. I cannot but think God holds worldly wealth in light account, for those great men both died poor—but a nation's gratitude will make their memories rich forever.

The Hudson was the scene of MR. FULTON's first success; but he always said the Mississippi would behold his final triumph. His ardent aspirations were quenched by his early and lamented death; but the great river will bear witness forever to his genius.

The current of that stream swollen by its tributaries, which come rolling down from the broad declivities of the Alleghany and Rocky Mountains, was so strong as nearly to destroy its value for the purposes of commerce. Its ascent, from New-Orleans to the territory north of the Ohio, unaided by steam, often required from two to three months. MR. FULTON's invention reduced it to four days.

It was that great victory over Nature, virtually annihilating time and space, and equalizing the condition of the population of that wide-spread valley, which has imparted to the Mississippi its highest attribute—its power to bind the vast communities on its banks in perpetual, political union.

The great object of the Constitution was, to nationalize the commerce and navigable waters of the United States, by uniting them all under a common authority, to be uniformly exercised, and it therefore expressly prohibited the separate States from interfering in any way with that authority. To any who may contend, that the States possess a concurrent authority which they may lawfully exercise, until it shall be superseded by the paramount power of the Union, we will merely answer that the authority of the Union, at any rate, becomes supreme when exercised.

The waters of New-York have furnished a signal evidence of this. The State Legislature, to reward MR. FULTON'S services, attempted to grant to him, for a term of years, the exclusive right of navigating the Hudson by steam. Connecticut and New Jersey immediately resisted. They passed laws of a hostile and even belligerent character, and the scenes of the Confederation and the Chesapeake seemed about to be repeated. A steamboat from New Jersey, bearing the significant name of the "*Bellona*," attempting to enter the limits of New York, was restrained by State authority; but its owner, as was well said on a similar occasion, "went not to war, *but to law*." The case was of transcendant importance, directly involving the supremacy of the Union over its navigable waters, and never did this country behold a greater display of intellectual vigor and forensic eloquence, than the four great combatants exhibited who were selected to vindicate, on that occasion, the right of the respective Governments, before the Supreme Court of the United States, with Chief Justice MARSHALL at its head.

The written opinion of that great jurist, in deciding this question, is a masterpiece of constitutional logic. It scattered to the winds every pretence of State authority, to interfere with the navigable waters of the Union, and established the national supremacy on a basis which nothing can shake.

And what course did New York pursue, on receiving this decision? Did she attempt to nullify—to secede—to assume the air and port of an offended Nation? Did she attempt to seize the Hudson, and go off with it out of the Union? No, my friends, she obeyed the law and the Constitution, and stands, where I trust she will always stand, a lofty example of national loyalty and dignified obedience.

And now we enter upon a curious portion of the history of our navigable waters. A mischievous political sect has arisen in our American world, which holds as a cardinal point of party faith, that the navigable waters of the Union are those only, in which the tides of the ocean ebb and flow.

This narrow notion originated in the common law of England, an island in which rivers, in our American sense, are not only unknown, but impossible. England, lying in a high northern latitude, its shores are washed by an ocean tide, which rises from twenty to thirty feet, and rushes into the numerous bays, which deeply indent the coast. Little streams there called "rivers," empty into these bays, but above the high-water mark imprinted by the tide, they have no navigation worthy of notice.

But how do streams like these compare with the Mississippi? More than a thousand miles above the mouth of that river, its waters can float a vessel of a thousand tons throughout the year. Above that point, it receives the Missouri, a stream so graphically described by WEBSTER,—not less poet than statesman,—as "coming down two thousand miles from among the savages, to imprint its barbarian character on the Mississippi!" Their accumulated waters frequently rise fifty feet above the summer level, and hurry downward to the Gulf, where they meet a languid ocean tide of eighteen inches! The average volume of water, throughout the year, at the river's mouth, exceeds in cubic contents, nearly three-fold that of the cataract of Niagara, and often pushes out the ocean tide for many miles. Now is it reasonable, that these English tide-water notions of navigable rivers shall be applied on this side of the Atlantic? Shall the little rivulets of England give law to a Continental river like ours? And nevertheless petty politicians, small men with smaller ideas, do take their law from England, and for years have contended, and some even yet contend, that in the eye of the American Constitution, the Mississippi, above the ocean high-tide water mark —if any such mark there be,—is not a navigable river, nor subject, as such, to the national authority.

Now, was not this enough to make a whole people go to war? But they did not, and again they went to law. Once more the authority of the Supreme Judicial tribunal of the Union was invoked—and during the year 1851, and not until then, was it finally established that the narrow rules, drawn from the English rivers, were not applicable to our navigable streams. Cobwebs and abstractions were swept away, and navigable waters were decided by Chief Justice TANEY, to be waters that could be navigated. One Judge only dissented, and he came from Virginia—of course.

The tide-water question being thus disposed of, let us ask, do the navigable waters of our great rivers and lakes, in fact, constitute channels of "commerce with foreign nations, and among the several States?"

Now, as to foreign commerce, it is very difficult to say, not where it begins, but where it stops. Cargoes may be shipped from Nova Scotia directly to Chicago or from Vera Cruz directly to Pittsburg. In such case, they pass through several States, on their way to the point of destination.— Surely such cargoes are sufficiently foreign to be furnished with harbors, or protected from snags on their way; and even if the steamboat bound for Pittsburg should be stopped by its owner on its way up the Ohio, and sent into the Wabash, the character of the commerce would remain unaltered.— Or, to take a case nearer home; vessels from Nova Scotia may constantly be seen ascending the Hudson, as far as Albany, and above the "*Overslaugh*," upon which so much constitutional argument has been expended.

But even if difficulties could be found, in determining the precise point in the interior, where "commerce with foreign nations" ceases to retain that character, there surely can be none in ascertaining the meaning of the term " commerce among the States."

For here again the Mississippi is at hand. The products of no less than sixteen States which now lie in its valley, are daily intermingled on its waters. If this is not commerce "among" the States, we may well despair of finding an instance. For let us look a little more minutely into the interior, and see what the people are about. Not to mention their vast interchanges,—iron sent from Tennessee two thousand miles to Pittsburg, and returned, manufactured, two thousand miles more,—or pine timber from South-western New York, finding its way to the Upper Mississippi,—is there a nook or corner in the whole valley so remote, that merchandise does not reach it from this our own city? Has it a navigable stream so small, that it is not at this moment bearing on its waters, the fabrics of the very manufacturers and mechanics I see about me? And cannot we all see, and feel how vital is our interest in the proper regulation and safety of such a commerce? Why, it is the very life blood of the system, flowing through every artery and vein, and invigorating the body politic to its remotest extremities.

Nor is the interest of such a question confined to our commercial cities. Where in all the wide-spread West, is there a hamlet so small, that it does not consume the cotton, the sugar, and the tobacco of the South—the sunny South—stretching away from the Chesapeake, around Cape Florida to the Rio Grande?—or the thousand and one manufactures of New-England? Do not wooden clocks from good old Connecticut, try the temper of the woodsmen of Minnesota? Why, the very oysters, now eaten at the falls of St. Anthony, are first carried from their ocean bed in New-Jersey, through the long concatenation of rivers, and railroads, and canals, and lakes, and railroads again, which stretch more than a thousand miles from the Atlantic to the Mississippi; seasoned, too, with salt, river-borne from the interior of Virginia, and pepper, ocean-borne from the farthermost islands of Asia. And can we not, from these homely examples, perceive the universality of our inland commerce?

The statistical tables are beginning to furnish some little idea of its pecuniary value. The admirable report to the Senate of the United States by Colonel ABERT, Chief of the Topographical Engineers, made after very close and accurate investigation, estimates the annual trade of the Mississippi, for the year 1850, at two hundred and seventy-four millions of dollars, and for the year 1860, at four hundred and ninety-four millions. But what may we not expect, before the present generation shall pass away? Why, there are men now before me, who will see the annual movement on the Mississippi and its tributaries numbered, not by hundreds of millions, as at present, but by thousands of millions. And is not this "commerce among the States?" Is not a commercial movement like this,—a labor-saving machine working on a scale so vast—a God-given stream, thus developing, at every moment, elements of national strength and prosperity so gigantic, as well worthy the attention of our Government, as the barren and worthless abstractions, by which political fanatics seek to paralyze its powers?

The annual losses of boats and their cargoes, on the waters of the Mississippi, by "snags," sandbars, and similar obstructions, was estimated in the year 1846, by a Committee of the Senate of the United States, upon authentic data, to have been $2,601,200, and have doubtless kept pace since that time with the increase of the river commerce. We insist that the government of the Union is bound to exert every legitimate power it possesses, to prevent losses like these.

At the time of forming the Constitution, the common right of all the citizens of all the States to navigate the Mississippi and the Great Lakes was emphatically denominated a "RIGHT OF THE UNION," as contradistinguished from the right of any separate State. We claim that a RIGHT so sacred and fundamental, was accompanied by a DUTY equally sacred and fundamental. The States surrendered to the Union all revenue derived from commerce, and thus parted with the very means of facilitating the business, which produced that revenue. They parted too with the control of all the navigable waters, which furnished the channels for that commerce. The doctrine on this subject has been so clearly stated by an eminent fellow-laborer in our cause,* that I beg to quote his words: "The States," said he, "could never have intended to deliver themselves up to the care of the Federal Government, stripped of the means of securing the first elements of their prosperity, and thus manacled and fettered, without an equivalent. And what was that equivalent? The only one which the case admitted—the substitution of the Federal Government for the exercise of the powers, and the performance of those correlative duties, which the exigencies of the confederacy forbade to the States. In the very nature of things, the Federal Government took the place and received the powers, and thereby assumed those duties of the States respectively, which they could not separately exercise, consistent with the peace and prosperity of the whole. This was the great compromise of the Constitution."

The neglect of the Government to discharge the duty so plainly devolving upon it, is the more inexcusable, when we reflect how well it can afford to take care of the navigable waters committed to its charge. It took these great channels of intercourse, expressly subject to the burthens which Nature had imposed upon them—burthens bearing no sort of proportion to the benefits received. The whole sum hitherto expended on the Mississippi, and all its great tributaries—the Missouri, the Arkansas, the Red, the Cumberland, and the

* John C. Spencer.

Ohio Rivers—is less than three millions of dollars; and shall we begrudge that sum for a commerce counted by hundreds of millions?

It is the very magnitude of those streams which produces effects, which call for corresponding energy to counteract. It is their office to carry off the wash of more than half a continent—in doing which they sweep along not only the sands of the wide-spread plains, but immense masses of trees, which they uproot in their turbulent career, and strew along their way. Their channels, of course, become endangered, or, in the case of the "raft" of the Red River, obstructed altogether.

Now, we admit it to be no child's play to "curb the licentiousness of nature" when operating on a scale like this; but we claim that a Nation has been raised up by Providence strong enough to do it. The great NAPOLEON was once master of the largest portion of the valley drained by the Mississippi. Think you, if he had retained his portion he would not have swept from the channel every obstacle to its perfect navigation? How long would he have permitted sand bars and snags to disgrace the imperial river?

My friends, it is unbecoming the dignity of the American people, to permit this great national nuisance to continue. No other civilized nation, ancient or modern, known to mankind, has thus disgraced itself. Why, if we look back two thousand years ago, we find that the very first efforts of the great ALEXANDER of Macedon, in pouring Greek civilization into the valley of the Euphrates, were directed to the care and improvement of its navigation. Russia in these modern days most sedulously guards its rivers, and removes every obstruction from their icy currents. Several European monarchs unite, to keep the Rhine in navigable condition. AUGUSTUS, the master of the Roman world, deemed it his highest office to restrain the inundations of the Tiber. Controlled by his vigorous arm, that angry stream,

"Doctus iter melius,"

was taught to mend its ways. And cannot the whole American Union teach better manners to the Mississippi, and even to the "barbarian" Missouri? Republicans of America, Sovereigns of the New World—let us stand up to our work, and not allow empires or monarchies, old or young, to outdo us!

And now we must enter upon an inquiry of some perplexity, for we must discover, if possible, by what strange infatuation, the Government of the Union could have been induced to abandon or neglect a duty so honorable, so important, and so imperative,—and we must wander far away from our broad lands and waters, into the dreary regions and among the dreamy shadows of political abstraction.

These singular creations of the human brain would seem at first to be harmless—airy nothings—hardly deserving a local habitation or a name. And yet we shall find that, shadows as they are, they have for many years exerted, and still exert, a baneful interest over all the substantial interests of the American people, and in the hands of political jugglers have frightened the Government from its propriety, and almost stolen away the senses of the nation.

Before attempting to describe them, let us remark, for the fact is important, that none of them ever disturbed the administration of President JEFFERSON. So far from that, he fully carried out the practical policy which President WASHINGTON had commenced, of regulating commerce by light-houses and other facilities required for its safety and convenience—and superadded to that policy, as we have seen, the purchase of the port of New Orleans, and the territory of Louisiana.

Nor did Mr. JEFFERSON withhold similar facilities on the land, for in 1806 he commenced the Cumberland Road, to stretch from the Potomac through the territory of six of the States to the Mississippi—a work which, we may add, was continued under every succeeding administration until 1838, when, after an expenditure of nearly six millions, it came to its end under the Government of Mr. VAN BUREN.

In addition to these facilities within the jurisdictional limits of the United States, Mr. JEFFERSON commenced the survey of the Coast, which is even yet in progress: and that, too, for the express purpose, as avowed by the act of 1807, of making discoveries which might "be specially subservient to the *commercial interests* of the United States!" That act requires the survey to include not only "all the islands and shoals within twenty leagues of the shores of the United States," but also the soundings and currents out to the Gulf Stream—the great Ocean River, distant more than five hundred miles from the Coast.

Let no one, therefore, do Mr. JEFFERSON the injustice to believe, that he ever for a moment hesitated to exercise the power to regulate commerce, by affording it all needful physical facilities. It seems, however, that a discovery has been made by some of his pretended followers—who claim, *par excellence*, to be his most faithful disciples—that in after life, he expressed opinions at variance with these public official acts. To prove this, they produce extracts from his writings, purporting to contain certain phrases, which they now proclaim aloud, as the fundamental dogma of Jeffersonian Democracy. They are as follows:

"The world is *governed too much*. Government must protect every man in his life, liberty, and property, and *there stop*."

Now, whether Mr. JEFFERSON ever used these words in their unrestricted sense, or whether he explained or modified them by other expressions, we know not; but if he did so use them, we can only claim to gather his opinions from his acts and not his language.

The time would not suffice to point out a tithe of the mischiefs such a doctrine would inflict upon all the most valuable institutions of human society—its public schools—its public charities—its great institutions of learning—its public works of every description, in fact everything dear to civilization and humanity.

We have, however, seen but too plainly here in the North, the effects of this doctrine, in the hands of office-seeking demagogues, who parade it as the test of party faith. In New Hampshire in particular—it arrested or greatly retarded for several years, the progress of all public improvement—forbidding even the incorporation of companies with adequate powers. In our own New York, political leaders found in it the key to political power, which enabled them with ruthless hand, not only to arrest the enlargement of our great artificial channel of commerce—the pride and glory of the State—but to bind down the people by a Constitution which, if left unaltered, will postpone the work for a whole generation. Nay, more—it has enabled those leaders, aided by kindred spirits in the States around the lakes, to propagate similar constitutions through all that region, virtually disabling their State authorities from expending a dollar on public works. And then, after doing all this and after denying the power of the Nation to build harbors for the protection of commerce, they call in cruel mockery, upon the very States they have thus manacled, to construct the works!

And what do we see? The State of Michigan, permitted by the Government to take exclusive possession of the outlet of Lake Superior, and improve the Sault St. Marie, but weighed down by these chains, unable to stir an inch!

But if such a dogma has been mischievous in the separate States, how much more disastrous would be its effects, if applied to the Union! If indeed it be true that Government, after protecting every man in his life, liberty, and property, *must there stop*, why should we regulate commerce at all—still less by physical means?

But leaving this, the broadest of all political abstractions, we come down to a class, which merely denies to the National Government all practical power over the regulation of commerce.

And here we encounter one general abstraction, which seems to cover all this particular class. It is that the Government of the United States is not a Union, but only a Confederacy; in a word, that we are not a Nation, but merely a League of States absolutely sovereign; that the nation acts only on a grander scale, as common attorney for those sovereign States—each of which may judge of the extent of the powers granted—that the powers thus temporarily delegated to this "Confederacy" are strictly limited, and must be strictly construed; that the tribunals expressly provided by the Constitution have no authority to decide upon the extent of such limitation, but that the President, especially if elected by politicians holding these doctrines, has full power to narrow the exercise of the powers by Congress, to suit his own peculiar tenets.

And such has been the actual result. The American people by some magic have been induced to elect a succession of Presidents wedded to this particular political faith, and our great navigable waters have severely felt the results.

It is therefore necessary for us, if possible, to understand the nature of this particular class of abstractions. We shall find them somewhat difficult to define or comprehend, for they have every possible variety of form, color and extent. We may, however, succeed in stating some of them, and especially those which have done most harm to the country. They seem to be these:

1. That the power to regulate commerce, is merely the abstract power to regulate the duties to be imposed upon it—and to prohibit the States from imposing such duties.

2. That if the power exists at all to afford any physical facilities, it is limited to high-tide water mark.

3. That rivers cannot be improved above the " ports of entry" established by Congress.

4. That a river cannot be improved, if lying wholly within a State.

5. That it is not enough for a river to separate two States, but it must adjoin or pass through three at least.

6. That harbors constructed by the Government, must be harbors for shelter and not for commerce.

7. That if it is lawful at all to deepen our navigable waters, it is not lawful to place in them piers or any similar structures, as that would encroach on the territorial jurisdiction of a State and trespass on its "sovereignty."

8. That it is not lawful to remove obstructions in our navigable waters, but that it is lawful to erect beacons on those obstructions.

The last of this brilliant list, came into the political world during the administration of President Polk. Congress had ordered a beacon to be placed on a rock, in the harbor of New Haven. The engineer reported that the cost of removing the rock, would be less than the cost of erecting the beacon. But the President was firm. A great party doctrine was involved, and the rock remains to uphold the beacon—a naked pole with an empty barrel at its head —a suitable type of the whole class of constitutional abstractions.

It is important also to understand the historical progress of these abstractions, in enfeebling the authority of the nation. They did not make their appearance to any extreme extent, until near the close of the administration of General Jackson. On the contrary, during the eight years in which that eminent man controlled the affairs of the Government, its nationality was not materially impaired.

The sums expended during that time upon rivers and harbors, including the Cumberland road, and some other roads of minor extent, was between ten and eleven millions of dollars.

During his time, however, an opinion began to gain ground, that though it might be constitutional, it was not expedient for the national Government to construct turnpike roads within the limits of the States; but that works of that description, might better be left to the States, or to individuals incorporated by their authority. Gen. JACKSON therefore vetoed a bill, for building a turnpike from Maysville into the interior of Kentucky. He went a step further, and vetoed a bill for the improvement of the Wabash river, which being above any "port of entry," it was in his judgment, a local work.

Mr. VAN BUREN, who succeeded him in 1837, followed his footsteps so far only as to encourage the theories of the abstractionists; and the vagaries in which they indulged as to the legitimate power of the Government, soon gained a stronger foothold.

The improvements of rivers and harbors which had been commenced by Gen. JACKSON, Mr. VAN BUREN after a short time allowed to languish, and they finally came to an end, before the close of his Presidential term in 1841. But a valuable discovery was then made in party politics, for it was then well ascertained, that the true mode for Northern men to get the Southern votes necessary for attaining or retaining the Presidential chair was, resolutely to uphold the abstractions we have been considering.

The political party of Mr. VAN BUREN controlled both branches of Congress, and they adjourned without making any appropriations for rivers and harbors. But this was not quite enough. The South might fear that the works would be resumed at a subsequent session, and it was therefore necessary to offer up before the whole nation, some open and notorious sacrifice, which should stand as an unmistakeable pledge of political faith, and satisfy the whole American people, that every thought or hope of improving our navigable waters by national authority was permanently abandoned.

The Government of Mr. VAN BUREN accordingly issued orders, under which all the boats, machinery, and other apparatus which had been purchased at great expense for the construction of harbors on the Lakes, were publicly sold at auction.

Mr. VAN BUREN was succeeded by JOHN TYLER, in whose time abstractionism took a more distinct and malignant type, accompanied however, by some strange phenomena. A bill providing, among other things, for the improvement of certain harbors on the Atlantic, including the Delaware Breakwater, the improvement of the Hudson River near Albany, and the James River at Richmond, was vetoed by President TYLER on the ground, that each State possessed exclusive jurisdiction over all streams and water courses within its territorial limits;—and nevertheless he signed at the same time, another bill for improving the Ohio river and numerous harbors on the Western

Lakes, lying within the mouths of rivers, and for all constitutional purposes as much within the jurisdiction of the States, as the James river or the Hudson. The annual commerce, foreign and domestic, then existing on the Hudson river, and embarrassed by the obstructions which this vetoed bill might have removed, exceeded one hundred and fifty millions of dollars. A very remarkable reason was also given in the veto message, which added another to the abstractions above enumerated, and it was that the improvement of the James river at Richmond, by increasing the trade of that city, would correspondingly lessen that of Petersburgh! a principle which, if adopted, would stop every species of improvement, and compel us to leave the world in a state of nature.

In 1845, JAMES K. POLK succeeded Mr. TYLER. Coming from Tennessee, it was hoped that he would carry into the Government somewhat of the nationality of General JACKSON. But Mr. POLK exceeded all his predecessors, in the narrowness and severity of his theories. He not only vetoed the bills for continuing the harbors which had been commenced by General JACKSON, but he flatly denied all authority whatever in the national Government to expend money for any such objects—denouncing the whole as utterly unconstitutional.

The reasons he gave would equally include light houses and beacons. To be consistent, he should have vetoed them also, but they were allowed to stand,—at least for a time.

Mr. POLK did what was much worse. He brought forward a plan for the virtual division and dismemberment of all the navigable waters of the Union—the Mississippi, the Lakes, and all—and the abandonment of all authority to regulate their improvement by the national Government. The plan was distinctly proposed in an elaborate message, which recommended that Congress should at once give its consent in advance, that each State should levy tonnage duties on all vessels entering the harbors within its limits—to be applied to the improvement of the rivers and harbors within such limits, exclusively by the State, and in such manner as its local authorities should see fit—thus reproducing, at a stroke, the evils of the old Confederation—shivering to atoms the fabric which the Constitution intended to rear, and destroying those two great cardinal and prominent features—the unity and the freedom of our navigable waters—which distinguish America from all the other nations of the world.

On the 5th of July, 1847, a Convention of Delegates—to consider the condition of our navigable waters—from eighteen of the States, assembled at Chicago—a large commercial city in the heart of the continent, near the Southern extremity of Lake Michigan, and preëminently a fitting place for such an assemblage. General CASS, in the speech to which I have alluded, terms it, sneeringly, a "renowned Convocation." It was indeed renowned, as well in numbers as in weight of character and patriotic devotion to the country and its best interests, and, in all these respects, and above all, in the decent decorum of its proceedings, will stand a comparison with any public body ever assembled in America, not excepting Congress itself.

The interests of the country were greatly suffering. Our lakes and rivers were strewed with wrecks, which the cruel neglect of the Government had caused—and the sufferers spake out plainly. The place of meeting was immediately opposite the great peninsula of Michigan—a State of large and increasing commerce, and greatly needing safe and commodious harbors; and a State moreover, which had carried forward General CASS to wealth and greatness. He was respectfully invited to attend this Convention, but "circumstances" prevented him. What those circumstances were, were never publicly known, until his recent speech in the Senate, which distinctly avows, that he abstained from attending, because he "was satisfied that it was got up for the purpose of injuring Mr. POLK, *and through him the Democratic party.*"

I have no wish to comment upon this avowal, further than to observe that it establishes two important facts on the very best authority, the first of which is, that "the Democratic party" are thus distinctly identified with Mr. POLK, as enemies to the improvements in question;—and the second, that the power of the American President has indeed become dangerous, when a Senator of the United States, in a case where the interests of his State are vitally concerned, does not dare openly to disagree with the Executive, or take any efficient means to resist the abuse of his authority. It also shows the utter folly of electing to that office either an abstractionist or an ally of abstractionists, under the vain expectation that Congress will be able to restrain him from the tyrannical exercise of the veto power, with which the Constitution has clothed him. Experience has taught us too well, that in the power of the American President to resist all measures for the improvement of navigable waters, he is to all intents as much an autocrat as the Czar of Russia. And shall we, with our eyes open, enter upon another dynasty of misrule and folly?

The Chicago Convention appointed a Committee of two from each of the States represented in the Convention, to collect and embody information as to the trade of the Western waters, and the necessity for its more efficient protection, with a proper memorial, to be presented to Congress. The duty of preparing that important paper, vindicating the constitutional authority of the nation and the necessity for its exercise, was committed to JOHN C. SPENCER, of New York; and it is enough to say that his great powers were thrown wholly into the work. The masterly exposition which he then made, not only of the right and duty of Congress to improve our Rivers and Harbors, but of the utter fallacy, folly, and unconstitutionality of the proposed plan of

State tonnage duties, is one of the most valuable State papers ever produced in this country. Let our opponents answer it, if they can.

The scheme of State tonnage duties did not, after all, originate with Mr. Polk. The true author was John C. Calhoun, of South Carolina, who saw in it a plan peculiarly harmonizing with his views of State sovereignty, and well calculated to enfeeble the national authority. Shortly after the veto of Mr. Polk, Mr. Rhett, of S. C., introduced a bill into the House of Representatives, giving the consent of Congress to the local tonnage duties to be levied by the States. It was referred to the Committee of Commerce, of which Washington Hunt, the present Governor of the State of New York, was Chairman. Earnest efforts were used by Mr. Rhett, to point out to Governor Hunt, the peculiar advantages which New York would derive in levying local duties, from her geographical position, in holding the very gates of commerce, both on the Atlantic and the Lakes. But Washington Hunt was a National Whig, and loyal to the Constitution. It was enough for him, as it is for all good Whigs, that New York should be part of one great Republic. He scorned to seek, and would not accept advantages for his State by a measure that would weaken the Union; but presented to the House a report condemning the plan in the strongest terms. It took a broad and comprehensive view of our commerce, foreign and domestic, and the just right of every portion of the Union to be fairly protected, and placed on a proper national basis the duty which the government had so long neglected. It also reprobated the arbitrary veto, by which the President had defeated the Harbor Bill. The report was accompanied by four separate resolutions, upon which a vote was obtained in July, 1848, after a desperate resistance by the friends of the Executive.

The first resolution, asserting the power of the National Government to improve Rivers and Harbors, was passed by a vote of 128 to 59.

The second, asserting the expediency of exercising that power, was passed by a vote of 112 to 53.

The third, disapproving the veto of the President, was passed by 91 to 71.

And the fourth, condemning the proposed plan of State tonnage duties, was passed by 109 to 59.

It not being practicable to obtain two-thirds of the House to pass the Harbor Bill notwithstanding the veto, the bill failed, and our Lakes and Rivers were left to their fate.

In November of that year, Zachary Taylor was chosen President of the United States, and it was really believed to be impossible that this important national interest could be longer neglected. But such was the violence of party, or so great the fear of offending Southern abstractionists, that nearly four years elapsed before the Whigs could succeed in passing a River and Harbor Bill. Their opponents held majorities in both Houses, and steadily refused to pass it, until late in the summer of the present year, when the near approach of the Presidential election, and the apprehension of losing the votes of the States interested in internal navigation, operated to convince a sufficient number of the expediency of voting for the bill. It is almost needless to say that MILLARD FILLMORE, the Whig President, signed it without a moment's hesitation.

It must be obvious that this revival of the River and Harbor policy is only temporary, and will again be abandoned unless the people can succeed at the approaching election in placing a Whig in the Presidential chair. We have seen the baleful effects, of placing in that position an abstractionist, or Northern ally of abstractionists. What can we possibly expect if we elect any but a Whig? It is already distinctly announced by the political press of Virginia—which has the merit, at least, of openness and candor—that General PIERCE, if elected, will abandon the policy just renewed. Now can we, will we consent that the protecting arm of the Government shall again be paralyzed?

But this is not all—for there is a feature in the approaching contest, which gives it a much higher and more enduring interest. The success of our opponents will permanently fasten upon the nation a plan of local tonnage duties, even more mischievous and destructive than that which Mr. POLK proposed.

During the recent struggle to pass the River and Harbor Bill through the Senate, Mr. DOUGLAS of Illinois, offered as a substitute, an amendment, giving the consent of Congress to the levy of local tonnage duties, not only by each of the separate States, but even by the authorities "*of any city or town,*" on the whole extent of the coasts of the Atlantic, the Pacific, the Gulf of Mexico and all the Lakes, and further allowing any of the States, either singly or by compact among themselves, to levy similar duties on all the navigable rivers of the Union, within their respective limits. The plan of President POLK divided the national waters of the Union, into only thirty-one separate portions —while that of Senator DOUGLAS subdivides them into as many parts, as there are towns on the whole ocean and lake coasts. Can it need any comment? Where could it find a parallel? In its utterly denationalizing effects, its daily and hourly checks, delays, exactions, and imposition, it would exceed even the subdivision of the waters of Europe, among the crowds of petty States and feudal barons, after the dismemberment of the Roman Empire; and America in the middle of the nineteenth century, would enjoy the singular privilege of inverting the whole course of modern civilization, and returning to the barbarism of the dark ages. Our coasts and rivers would be lined with collectors, demanding tribute. Vessels from Pittsburg to New Orleans would be stopped at least nine times on their voyage. Pretended improvements would be made or attempted wholly unsuited to their object, and other improvements omitted that commerce demanded. Agricultural States would hesitate or refuse to execute the works, which their more commercial neighbors required. The younger or smaller States would shrink from the burthen, while the States around the Lakes, manacled by their so-called " democratic " Constitutions would be totally disabled. States making trifling improvements would exact the same tribute, as those which were burthened with the most costly. Nothing like uniformity of plan would be practicable, while the due application of the duties would be a subject of interminable discussion and strife. Truly was it said by the Chicago memorial, that "if the wit of man were taxed to devise a scheme utterly destructive of all trade, commerce, and navigation upon our waters, a better one for the purpose than this, of artificially obstructing them by hosts of collectors of tonnage duties imposed by local legislation could not be framed."

But in addition to all this, the measure would be utterly unconstitutional, in violating the fundamental provision of the great Ordinance of 1787, the obligation of which was assumed by the Constitution, and which declared the Mississippi, the St. Lawrence, and all their tributaries, to be " common highways, and FOR EVER FREE,*without any tax, impost, or duty therefor*." Nor would it stop even here. It would come in direct conflict with the fundamental conditions contained in the five several acts admitting into the Union the States of Louisiana, Arkansas, Missouri, Iowa, and Wisconsin, each of which came into the Union under the express condition, that the Mississippi and its tributaries should remain forever free, without any tax, duty, or impost to be levied *by said States.*

It is true that the proposed amendment of Mr. DOUGLAS was not adopted. The Presidential election was too near at hand—but he has given notice, that he will renew it at the next session of Congress. If any think it impossible that such a measure can be adopted, let him remember that although its mischiefs and absurdities were pointed out in the strongest manner by Mr. TRUMAN SMITH, one of the Whig Senators from Connecticut—whose manly and vigorous speech on that occasion, deserves the thanks of every man engaged in inland commerce,—it nevertheless received the votes of seventeen Senators, among whom stands conspicuous Mr. WILLIAM R. KING, of Alabama, now nominated by our opponents for Vice-President of the United States, and presented to the people on the same ticket with GENERAL PIERCE. Can any one doubt the political character of their administration should they be elected? or the results which will follow to our navigable waters?

I have thus endeavored to bring down the history of this question to the present point, in order to ascertain what is the present attitude of the two contending parties. Our opponents with characteristic adroitness, have labored to blind the eyes of the country to the true issue. The resolution adopted by the Whigs at the Presidential Convention, which nominated SCOTT and GRAHAM, is open and explicit. It is this.

"The Constitution vests in Congress the power to *open and repair harbors, and remove obstacles from navigable rivers;* and it is expedient that Congress shall exercise that power whenever such improvements are necessary for the common defence, or for the protection and facilities of commerce with foreign nations, or among the States,—such improvements being, in every instance, *national and general* in their character."

Now, how do our opponents meet this resolution? I do not ask how they meet it by acts—for those we see—but how do they meet it by words? The resolution passed by the Presidential Convention which nominated PIERCE and KING, is in these words:

"The Constitution does not give the power to Congress to commence and carry on a *general system of internal improvements*"

The crafty and evasive character of the resolution is obvious. Its true object is to cajole the North, while it satisfies the South. On the one hand, it induces the North to believe that the party do not object to works strictly national, but only to roads, canals, and other similar works strictly local, and to a "*General System of Internal Improvement,*" only because it includes such local works—while, on the other hand, it satisfies the South that the phrase "internal improvements" includes all works of improvement, whether local or national.

But the practical effect on river and harbor improvements is precisely the same, as if the power to make these works was openly and distinctly denied by our opponents. This skillfully-worded resolution was first introduced in the Presidential Convention of 1840, which nominated Mr. VAN BUREN; and his followers have carefully stereotyped and repeated it, at every Presidential Convention from that time to the present. Under its equivocal phraseology, Mr. POLK found himself sufficiently justified in his vetoes, and should General PIERCE be elected, he will undoubtedly find it equally accommodating.

Now, we utterly deny that the Whig party contend for the doctrine that Congress has power to carry on a "general system of internal improvement." What they do contend for, is precisely this: That Congress has power to *open and repair harbors, and remove obstacles from navigable rivers.*

In respect to a "system" we claim, that Congress may, or may not pursue a systematic policy in respect to rivers and harbors, as they may in respect to any other subject of legislation. Surely, works which are national and constitutional in themselves, do not cease to be so, merely because they may be constructed in a systematic manner, or on a systematic plan. The Chicago memorial meets this whole matter in these few sentences:

"But we hear it said that the Constitution does not confer on Congress the power to regulate commerce, by commencing and carrying on a general system of internal improvement; as if the objection was not to any particular work, but to a general system. We confess our inability to perceive the force of this distinction. If any particular work can be justified by the importance of the commercial exigency which demands it, is not the power of Congress to facilitate commerce by any other similar work admitted? And if any work, in the judgment of Congress, possesses the requisites to bring it within the constitutional provision, does it cease to possess them because the commercial facilities it affords, may be augmented by its connection with other kindred works? Thus, the commercial cargoes, which now descend from Lake Michigan to the ocean, in their passage meet successively, the flats on Lake St. Clair, in the harbor of Buffalo, and in the overslaugh of the Hudson. The works needed to remove those three separate impediments, each highly necessary in itself, will be still more useful when all are completed, and when constructed, will naturally and necessarily group themselves together, and become portions of a system. But does this afford any reason, why each particular work should not be constructed? On the contrary, does it not greatly strengthen the inducement for building them all, and that too on a harmonious plan, so that each portion may add to the value of the whole?"

It is now more than twenty years since any one thought of a general system of *internal improvement* to be prosecuted by the national government. On the contrary, the separate States or corporations acting under their authority, have executed all works of internal improvement purely local. The States are overspread with a network of railroads more than ten thousand miles in extent, which have cost more than three hundred millions, not to mention the local canals, which have cost nearly one hundred millions more. All the States ask is, that the national Government may take care of the national waters—that, while the States are doing so much for the Union, the Union may do a little for itself. The total expenditure up to the present moment, extending over a period of forty years, is only seventeen millions of dollars; and yet attempts are made to alarm the country with the idea, that ruinous sums will be required. The amount expended on the Mississippi, the Ohio, and the Missouri, is less than three millions. The Cumberland road cost about six millions,—leaving only eight millions, as the sum total expended by the Government since its organization, upon other internal improvements of every description. Of this eight millions, $5,700,000 were expended upon harbors and breakwaters on the Atlantic and the Lakes, and $1,300,000 in improving navigable rivers, such as the Hudson, the Cape Fear, and the Savannah. Will any one pretend that the American Union cannot afford to expend sums like these, upon objects like these?

Why, gentlemen, a private company, a mere handful of individuals, in our city, have expended twenty-five millions in building the Erie Railroad, and our State another twenty-five in building and in part enlarging the Erie Canal,—while in Illinois, a State hardly thirty years old, another company is expending twenty millions in a railroad, to connect Lake Michigan with the mouth of the Ohio. It is possible, that in looking over the Union, we may find two isolated cases of canals,—to wit, one at the Falls of the Ohio, and the other at the Sault St. Marie, in which the general interest and the common security may require the nation to execute and control the work. But with those two exceptions, I know of no canal, or road, or local work, of any description, East of the Mississippi, which any Whig supposes should be constructed by the General Government. What then, do our opponents mean by their phrase—"A general system of Internal Improvements," except to deceive the people?

Stripped of all party disguise, the naked questions before the country are these, and only these:—

Shall THE NATION improve the NATIONAL NAVIGABLE WATERS, or leave them unimproved?

Will THE UNION preserve unimpaired the UNITY AND FREEDOM of its navigable waters, secured by the constitution, or will it surrender back those waters to the separate States, to be subjected to local authority and local impositions?

It is indeed, matter of serious concern, that questions like these, so vitally interwoven with our highest national interests, affecting so deeply, not only our present prosperity, but the welfare of the boundless Future which Providence has spread before us, should depend upon the varying issues of our party conflicts. But such, unhappily, is the fact; and we cannot, wisely or safely, close our eyes upon the momentous responsibilities which it imposes.

One word, and but a word, in conclusion, as to party epithets. Our opponents arrogate to themselves the exclusive use of the term "democracy." But it belongs much more tous than them. For what is democracy, but the equalization of human condition? and where can the world furnish equalizing agents more truly democratic, than cheap, rapid, and commodious channels of intercourse? They produce equality, not only among men of every rank and condition, but even among States and nations. The steam-engine on land and water, carries rich and poor alike. Canals transport their property alike. Rivers and harbors cleared from obstructions, and guarded from dangers, benefit all alike. They do more. They equalize the conditions of great communities of men. The great series of channels, natural and artificial, from the Atlantic to the Mississippi, not only place the County of Erie side by side with the County of Albany, but the State of Iowa side by side with the State of New-York.

On the distant Pacific, this nation possesses an almost boundless store of metallic wealth. Our young Democrats, full of energy and life, are striving to reach it. If we had the power to construct a road, which would carry them safely, cheaply and quickly, and give them equal access with their more favored countrymen to the common treasure—would not such a work be equalizing and democratic in its effects? And yet if we should dare to hint that Missouri with BENTON at its head, should be aided by all constitutional means in executing a work so truly necessary to the nation—equalizing the condition of the Continent, placing Pacific by the side of Atlantic America, and thus riveting the great bond of our continental union—would not a whole army of Abstractionists be let loose at once?

My friends, let us not be misled by party names, nor discouraged by party clamor—let us seek out our duty, and faithfully do it. Let us remember, that our generation comes early in the nation's history. Its shadow, lengthened by the morning light, will fall far beyond the scanty span of our narrow existence. Events are crowding quickly on us. It is no time to enfeeble the nation's powers. Seeing what is at stake, let us commit its guidance to men like the wise and far-seeing patriots, who framing our noble constitution, could discern the seeds of empire in the young republic—men possessing energy to direct the present, and wisdom to discern the future.

www.ingramcontent.com/pod-product-compliance
Lightning Source LLC
LaVergne TN
LVHW020741120826
845150LV00010B/2295

* 9 7 8 1 4 1 8 1 9 4 8 0 2 *